THE MIDNIGHT REVERIE

Dreamy Poetry and Prose

Written by:
Brandy Lane

Fort Wayne, Indiana

© 2025 The Midnight Reverie; A Poetry Collection

Author: Brandy Lane

Published in the United States of America by:

Where Beautiful Inks LLC
Fort Wayne, Indiana

ISBN: 978-1-970359-02-2

Library of Congress Control Number: 2025925670

All decorative art throughout this book is
through Canva and Canva Pro memberships with use of AI for some
elements of illustrations.
All prompts from Where Beautiful Inks LLC

DEDICATION

For my darling dragon—
the one who guards my quiet fire
and walks beside me through every darkened wood.
Your strength, your heat, your unyielding spirit
lit the path that became this book.

May these pages carry the echo
of your wings,
your roar,
your love—
the magic that keeps me brave.

BRANDY

Table of Contents

AUTHOR'S NOTE

The Midnight Reverie was born in the quiet hours—those rare moments when the world exhales and the forest begins to speak. I have always believed that night holds its own kind of truth, a language written in phosphorescent threads and wingbeats, in the soft pulse of bioluminescent mushrooms and the hush of creatures who dare to love in the dark.

This book is my attempt to follow that glow.

I wrote these pages while imagining a world where light does not come from the sun but from within—where moths carry secrets on their wings, where roots remember, and where love blooms in the shadows as fiercely as it does in daylight. These poems are wanderings, confessions, and small constellations gathered from the forest floor. They are for anyone who has ever felt illuminated by something delicate and inexplicable.

Thank you for stepping into the night with me. May you feel the tremor of your own reverie stirring beneath each line, and may the glow that guides you never dim.

BRANDY LANE

THE MIDNIGHT REVERIE

Dreamy Poetry and Prose

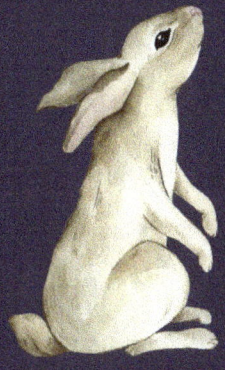

SEPULCHER BLOOM

Some gardens wake only in darkness—
where roots feed on the sinew of stars,
and petals unfurl like secrets too long kept.
The air sings a low requiem,
and every leaf remembers the taste of life.

I have wandered through halls of rot and radiance,
where moss devours forgotten altars,
and fungi shimmer like ghostlight on stone.
Even the silence has weight—
it presses against the sternum,
a pulse too slow to name.

Owls move as omens through the gloom,
their wings whispering elegies to the dead,
and beneath their flight, the earth exhales decay—
it's breath cold as confession,
it's hunger, infinite.

Sometimes, I think of you here—
your name, a contagion in my throat,
a prayer half-swallowed by shadow.

Would you know me still,
if we met in this silence between heartbeats—
this place where even stars forget to shine?

For the soil dreams of resurrection,
but only through decay.

And I—
I would offer you my shadow once more,
to bloom for you in darkness,
beautiful, even through death and ruin.

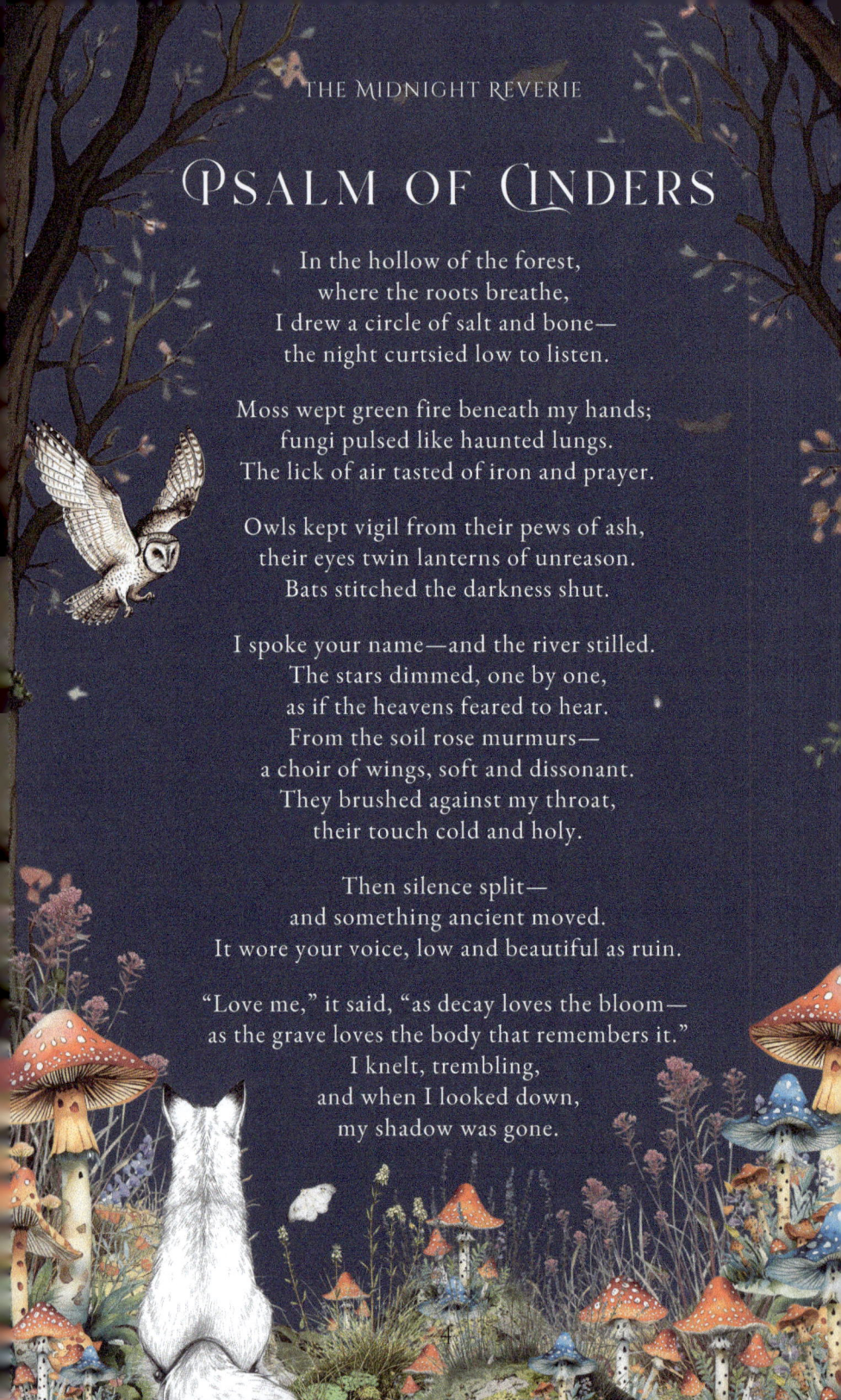

Psalm of Cinders

In the hollow of the forest,
where the roots breathe,
I drew a circle of salt and bone—
the night curtsied low to listen.

Moss wept green fire beneath my hands;
fungi pulsed like haunted lungs.
The lick of air tasted of iron and prayer.

Owls kept vigil from their pews of ash,
their eyes twin lanterns of unreason.
Bats stitched the darkness shut.

I spoke your name—and the river stilled.
The stars dimmed, one by one,
as if the heavens feared to hear.
From the soil rose murmurs—
a choir of wings, soft and dissonant.
They brushed against my throat,
their touch cold and holy.

Then silence split—
and something ancient moved.
It wore your voice, low and beautiful as ruin.

"Love me," it said, "as decay loves the bloom—
as the grave loves the body that remembers it."
I knelt, trembling,
and when I looked down,
my shadow was gone.

BRANDY LANE

PHOSPHOR BLOOM

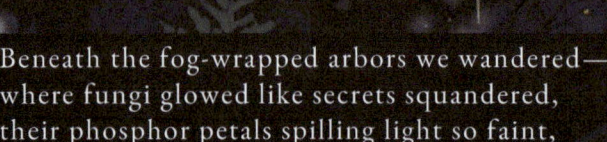

Beneath the fog-wrapped arbors we wandered—
where fungi glowed like secrets squandered,
their phosphor petals spilling light so faint,
a pale confession no night could taint.

A spectral fox slinked between shadow and root,
its eyes; twin lanterns in the velvet moot.
We traced the air with hands that never touched,
our breath a whisper, our hearts were clutched.

The wind hummed low, a hymn to the unseen,
and every shadow shimmered with emerald sheen.
We moved in cadence, a silent rhyme,
folding our devotion into the dark of time.

Through the garden of blackened stone we crept,
where dew-laced ferns curled while the night slept.
Fireflies winked like gems in the mire,
their light a tremor, a flicker of desire.

A serpent of shadow coiled around the root,
its scales gleaming with persimmon fruit.
We whispered vows that no tongue could tell,
and the earth beneath us chimed like a bell.

Phosphorescent tendrils twined our hands,
ribbons of light that pulsed through the lands.
Every heartbeat echoed a rhyme unseen,
every glance a covenant, quiet and keen.

Below a moon like molten pewter we lay,
where ash and smoke wove through the fey.
Bioluminescent vines spiraled and wound,
casting a net of shadow upon the ground.

Fire beetles blinked in a rhythmic rhyme,
trailing sparks through the folds of time.
Our fingers brushed—not upon flesh, but air,
tangling our spirits in a ritual rare.

The night exhaled in incense and loam,
folding us deep in its earthen home.
Every sigh became a spectral tune,
and love itself danced beneath that silvered moon.

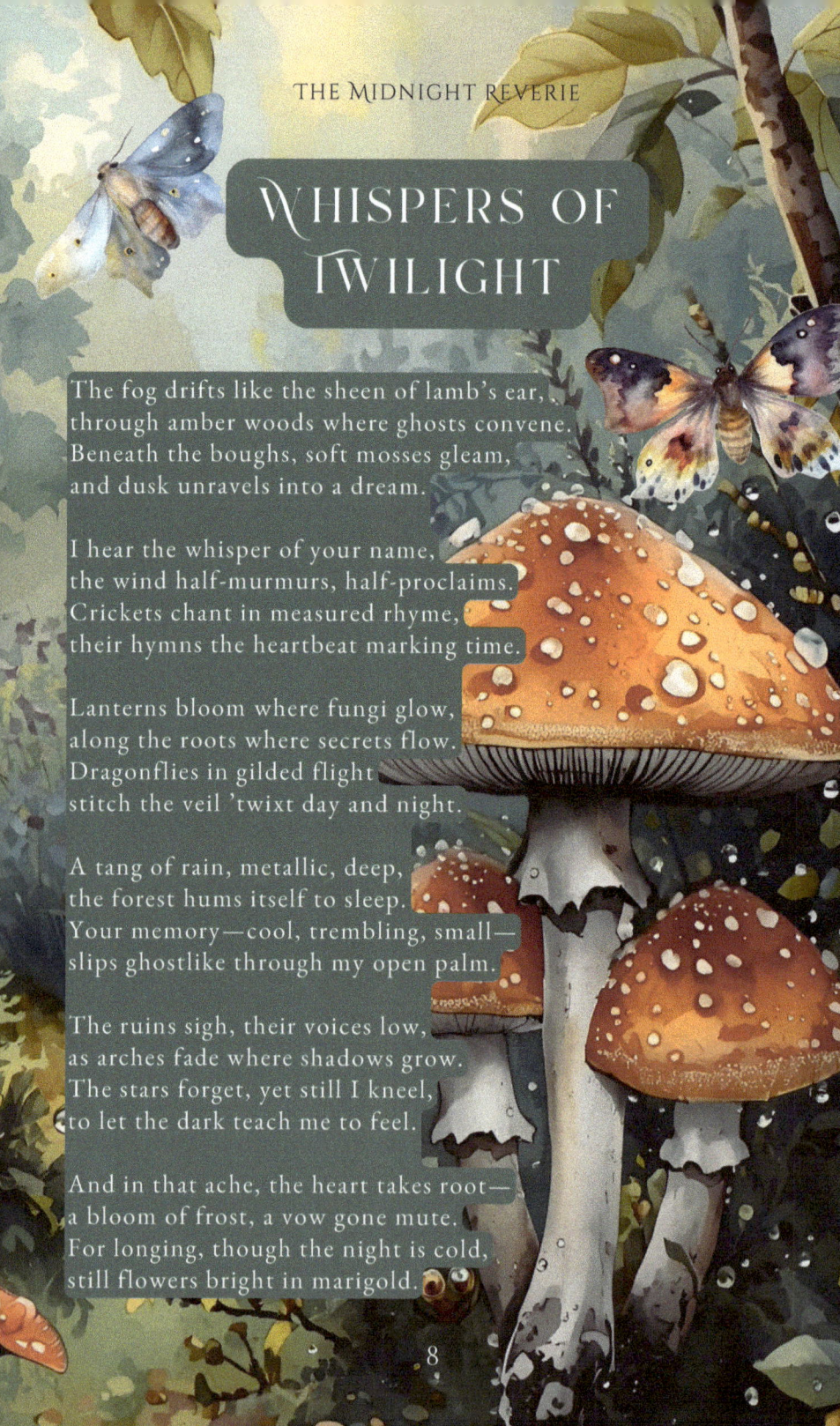

WHISPERS OF TWILIGHT

The fog drifts like the sheen of lamb's ear,
through amber woods where ghosts convene.
Beneath the boughs, soft mosses gleam,
and dusk unravels into a dream.

I hear the whisper of your name,
the wind half-murmurs, half-proclaims.
Crickets chant in measured rhyme,
their hymns the heartbeat marking time.

Lanterns bloom where fungi glow,
along the roots where secrets flow.
Dragonflies in gilded flight
stitch the veil 'twixt day and night.

A tang of rain, metallic, deep,
the forest hums itself to sleep.
Your memory—cool, trembling, small—
slips ghostlike through my open palm.

The ruins sigh, their voices low,
as arches fade where shadows grow.
The stars forget, yet still I kneel,
to let the dark teach me to feel.

And in that ache, the heart takes root—
a bloom of frost, a vow gone mute.
For longing, though the night is cold,
still flowers bright in marigold.

TWILIGHT'S EVE

Amber drips through trembling leaves,
a hush before the stars awake;
your laughter shivers through the eaves.

A firefly drifts, its silver wake
a thread that binds your heart to mine,
through fog that breathes, through fern and brake.

The crickets hum their small design,
the frogs respond in velvet song,
our shadows blur, our hands align.

Beneath the boughs where dreams belong,
the air tastes sweet as cider wine,
and time forgets both right and wrong.

Your gaze ignites the dark divine,
the night grows tender, flushed, complete—
its pulse now echoing with mine.

MIDNIGHT REVERIE

Midnight drapes herself over my shoulders—
a cloak stitched from shadow and longing.
Your voice calls to me, a silver thread,
pulling me into secret places
where the stars dare not wander.

Luna moths flutter against my skin,
their soft wings, vibrating,
their glow a whisper of what lingers
when desire becomes devotion.

I trace your absence along the earth,
feeling the pulse of hidden veins,
and the soil answers—soft, patient, eternal—
as if it, too, remembers our touch.

BRANDY LANE

WHERE SHADOWS BREATHE

The night unspools in threads of gray,
the stars fall dim, then fade away.
Beneath the roots, the quiet thrums—
a promise kept of what to become.

The roses rot, their scent still sweet,
their ghosts bloom pale 'neath my feet.
The wind recalls your final breath
and hums the lullaby of death.

Yet in that hush, the soil sings,
of ash reborn, of tender things.
Of seeds that split where sorrow lies,
and drink the tears the earth denies.

Your spirit moves within the loam,
a pulse, a whisper, finding home.
And every leaf that turns to flame
still bears the memory of your name.

So let the darkness close its eyes,
for even grief must learn to rise.
And in the hush where endings blend—
the heart begins again, my friend.

LUMINOUS ABYSS

From the yawning chasm from whence we came,
black holes murmur of our undoing—
their gravity, a lullaby of vanishing.
I wonder if our shadows might dissolve there,
like dust from some long-abandoned crypt?

In the sable dell of night—
where stars compete in crystalline fire,
bioluminescent mushrooms throb like buried hearts,
glow worms trace the secret veins of the earth,
and Luna moths flit on diaphanous wings—
cascading on sighs in the cool night air.

Rivers of starlight run through the trees,
and in the dimmest corners,
the night-blooming creatures move unseen—
their rituals older than grief,
older than the first poem ever written.

I would lie with you among the phosphorescent ferns—
our breaths a duet of laughter and song;
the world bending to the curve of our quiet,
as if the universe itself had paused
to watch—two hearts syncopated in the dark.

BRANDY LANE

MIDNIGHT GLOW

Canopied by the ebon of night—
where moonlight drips like molten silver,
moss-clad stones exhale damp secrets,
and roots spiral through the living earth.

From the hidden fissures whence we came,
the world whispers of collapse—
its pulse slow, deliberate—
pulling us toward some silent undoing.

I imagine our shadows dissolving
into the marrow of the soil—
a quiet return to darkness.

The midnight moths brush against bark—
their wings, almost black,
soft as the spaces between heartbeats.
Hoot owls, and bats—hungry for insects,
use keen eyes and silent talons, tracing the unseen.

Luminescent fungi wind through the underbrush—
casting an eerie, ghostly glow
on the creatures that haunt the night—
their routines carved by time,
more rare than bottled dragon's tears.

Here is where I press close to you—
as we breathe encapsulated dusk and hush,
the world narrowing to this secret grove,
as if the night itself craves to cradle us.

THE GHOST OF YOU

The stars have begun to dim—
their cold fire, bleeding through
the blackness of night.
I trace the outline of your absence
with hands that remember everything.

Winds carry your name like smoke—
ribboning through trees, through stone,
through memory.
Every echo boomerangs back onto me—
a hymn of what cannot be held.

Moths brush my cheek, wings soft as sighs.
They are light, diaphanous, fragile.
They gather in the spaces we left behind—
between heartbeats, between worlds.

I speak to you in silence—
a canticle of fading,
a vow for the vanishing,
and somewhere, far above,
the universe holds its breath to listen.

If you were here, the night would split open—
revealing all the hidden rivers of desire
that we let slip through our fingers.
But even apart, we resonate—
your shadow, and mine, entwined
in the endless dark.

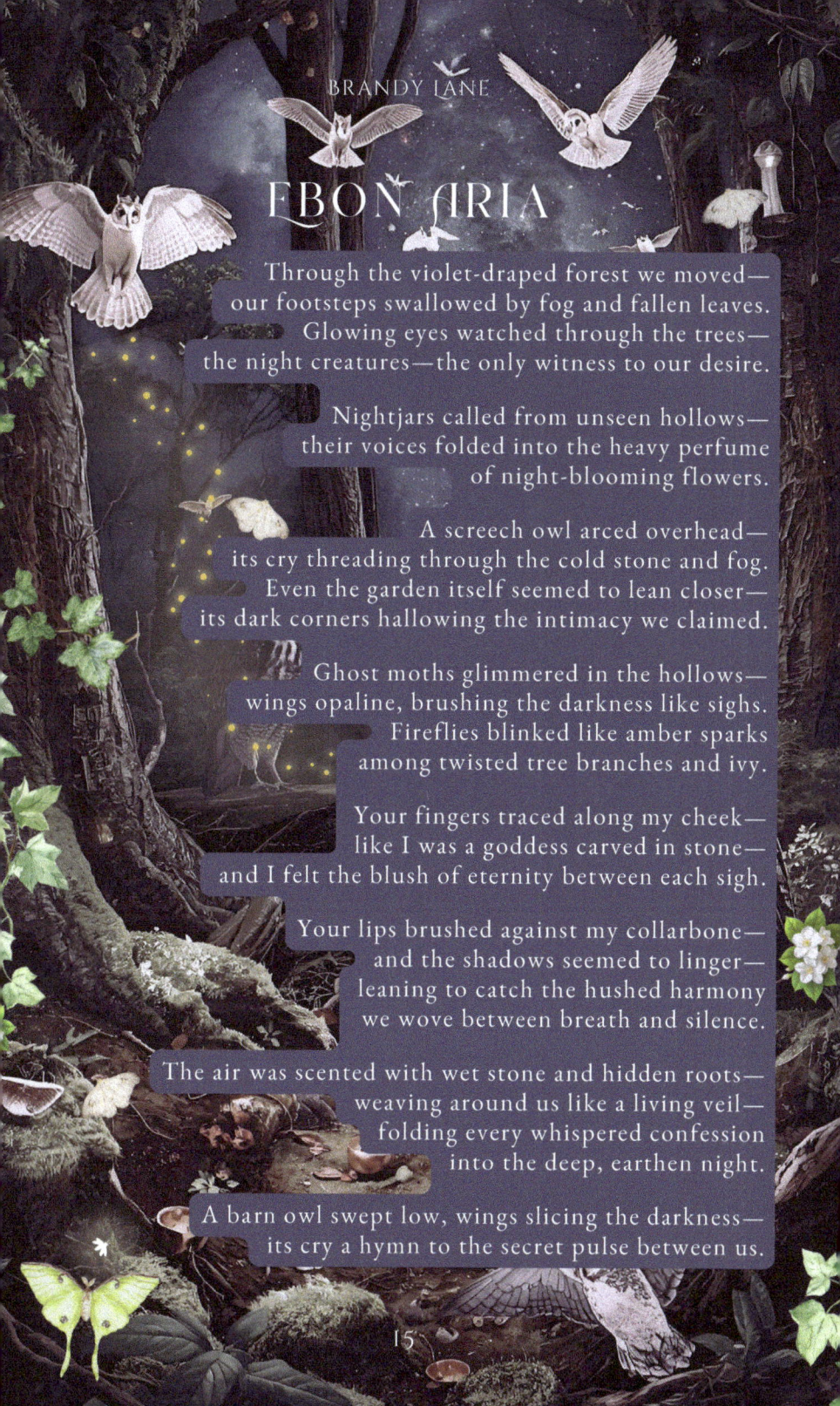

EBON ARIA

Through the violet-draped forest we moved—
our footsteps swallowed by fog and fallen leaves.
Glowing eyes watched through the trees—
the night creatures—the only witness to our desire.

Nightjars called from unseen hollows—
their voices folded into the heavy perfume
of night-blooming flowers.

A screech owl arced overhead—
its cry threading through the cold stone and fog.
Even the garden itself seemed to lean closer—
its dark corners hallowing the intimacy we claimed.

Ghost moths glimmered in the hollows—
wings opaline, brushing the darkness like sighs.
Fireflies blinked like amber sparks
among twisted tree branches and ivy.

Your fingers traced along my cheek—
like I was a goddess carved in stone—
and I felt the blush of eternity between each sigh.

Your lips brushed against my collarbone—
and the shadows seemed to linger—
leaning to catch the hushed harmony
we wove between breath and silence.

The air was scented with wet stone and hidden roots—
weaving around us like a living veil—
folding every whispered confession
into the deep, earthen night.

A barn owl swept low, wings slicing the darkness—
its cry a hymn to the secret pulse between us.

CATHEDRAL OF ASH

The mist shimmers in the moonlight,
the reflective light transcending the dark.

Longing hangs heavy in the air.
I kneel before the ruins of your shadow,
chanting every sigh you left behind.

Bats spiral above like inked prayers,
their wings slicing through silence.
Even the moon eavesdrops,
its silver cold on my upturned face.

Here, devotion is a litany of fog,
every exhale a secret, every heartbeat a psalm.
And when I whisper your name,
the ashes stir—
remembering what we dared to become.

BRANDY LANE

VELVET ECLIPSE

I found you beneath the weeping moon—
her silver tears pooling in the hollow of the garden.
The roses had wilted to crumbles,
but your gaze set them abloom again,
a secret fire that whispered only to me.

The night air thick with amber, and longing.
The owls circled above, their eyes, lanterns of quiet witness,
while the wind murmured in forgotten tongues,
folding around our bodies like a prayer.

Your hands traced the curve of my spine—
slow, deliberate, like a ritual forgotten by time.
I quivered beneath the press of shadow and silk,
each breath a confession we could not speak aloud.

We kissed as if the world might vanish in the next exhale,
and for a moment, it did—
crimson sparks drifted through the night,
and even the darkness bowed to us,
leaving only the blush of love in its wake.

LITANY OF VANISHING

I count the moments between your breaths—
each one a candle dancing in the wind.
The shadows peer—hungry for our shape.

We walk through halls of silent stars—
their light twinkling like chanted vespers.
Every footfall echoes through the marrow of the night—
leaving impressions of grief where they have trodden.

Say my name—
and the trees sway.
Say my name again—
and the river rises to near-flood.

The wind carries secrets—
the soft hum of wings,
the soft fall of snow from the heavens.
I swallow your shadow into mine—
weaving it into the fabric of the dark.

And when you vanish—
I grieve over your absence,
a litany of everything we were—
every sigh, every tremor,
every heartbeat absorbed by the night.

The stars will not remember us—
nor the moon—nor the soil beneath our feet.
Only I will recite this prayer—
and somewhere, somewhere beyond sight—
it will linger—
two souls balancing on the edge of forever.

BRANDY LANE

OBSIDIAN BOUGHS

Beneath the obsidian boughs, we whispered—
hands entwined like vines around forgotten stone.
Under the jade-leaning moon, we lingered—
the garden, thick with moonflower and shadow.

Moths, pale as ghosted silk,
danced through the air, trailing faint green fire—
their fragile bodies brushing against our devotion.
And Atlas moths traced silent arcs above us,
their wings dusted with ghostly phosphor,
stitching the darkness with delicate light.

The air tasted of damp earth and dragon's blood—
a quiet incense that clung to our skin.
Winds carried the scents of petrichor and clover,
ribboning through the hollowed trees—
while the garden exhaled,
holding us in its eternal quiet.

Owls with fiery eyes perched on skeletal limbs,
watching our covenant unfold in the misty glade.
A long-eared owl swept past—
a spy poised to spill our secrets
hidden in the folds of the garden's gloom.

Your hand pressed to mine—warm, deliberate—
and the night seemed to coil around us,
each breath a hymn only we could intone.
Every word we spoke became a rite—
a promise folded into the hollows of the night,
and even the wind seemed to pause,
listening to the silent music of our hearts.

THE CHAPEL OF WHISPERING VINES

In the ivy-clad courtyard, mist hovers like whispered prayer,
the stones hum underfoot, their memory fastened to the earth.
Candles linger in niches, their flames quiver as if alive,
casting light that bends against the stained-glass saints.

The air tastes of rosebuds and curiosity,
and the faint sweetness of clover pressed to marble.
No choir sings here now, yet every arch and column listens,
the hollowed stones carrying secrets older than the garden itself.

Vines thread through pews and pillars,
their leaves glinting with dew like fragments of celestial tears.
A large chime waits in the tower, silent but ready,
its shadow poised above the altar like a sentinel.

Each footstep becomes a rite, each breath a quiet offering,
and the garden exhales around me,
enveloping me into its ancient rhythm—
its songs written in roots and curling tendrils.

Here, the world holds still, between dusk and dawn,
between devotion and decay. Even the wind bends to listen,
and the chapel murmurs back a hymn that needs no voice—
a prayer that carries the weight of eternity.

SANCTUARY OF FALLEN PETALS

The courtyard lies under twilight, draped in wine-dark shadows,
petals fall from unseen blooms, carpeting the stone in quiet fire.
Every arch and balustrade hums with memory,
echoing with the footfalls of those long gone.

Candleglow flickers across frescoed walls,
casting saints and angels into hesitant motion.
The scent of myrrh drifts through the air,
woven with the sweetness of overripe fruit and earth.

A fountain trickles unseen, its water murmuring secrets,
while ivy snakes along walls, tracing patterns older than devotion.
No voice disturbs this sacred hush,
yet the air is thick with expectation—
as if the garden itself waits for a rite forgotten.

Shadows coil beneath stone benches,
and arches gather the sighs of night,
folding them into the ancient cadence of brick and vine.
Each movement, each breath, becomes a communion
with time, with decay, with the quiet that hovers
between heaven and earth.

Even the stars seem to lean closer,
their cold light falling like blessing or accusation,
and I kneel among the fallen petals,
absorbing the hush,
allowing the chapel's breath to fold me into its eternal prayer.

The Consuming Sky

We lay beneath the weight of stars—
their dying light trembling above us,
ancient, exhausted, and cruelly beautiful.
The air was sweet with endings;
the constellations wept in silence.

I felt your pulse beneath my palm,
steady as a tolling bell.
Each breath between us thickened the night—
a slow surrender of flame to shadow.
Even the moon turned its face away,
as if it could not bear to see.

Beyond the horizon, galaxies bled—
their colors dragged into the black.
The universe devours itself quietly,
like a lover tasting what it cannot keep.
I wondered if that was how we would end—
not in violence, but in longing so deep
it swallowed the light.

Your hand found mine—
a tremor, then stillness.
Time folded around us,
the sky a cathedral of collapse.
I thought I heard the stars confess,
their voices burning through the dark:
to love is to consume, and be consumed.

And so we were—
two fading fires in the great forgetting,
our ashes scattered through the void,
still orbiting each other
in the silence after time.

BRANDY LANE

THE ETERNAL NOCTURNE

Night drapes herself across the world—
a widow veiled in stars.
Her silence hums like a cello string,
drawn taut between life and remembrance.

We are her quiet instruments—
hands trembling in devotion,
breath syncing with the pulse of the void.
Every sigh a requiem,
every kiss an unholy prayer.

The moon watches—unblinking, pale—
a sentinel to our undoing.
Even the shadows hesitate,
awed by the soft violence of your touch.

The air tastes of lilac and lightning—
sweet decay, holy ache.
You whisper, stay, and the word
unfurls like smoke in the cathedral dark.

Beneath us, the earth hums our names,
a chant of marrow and memory.
Above, the stars weep silver rain,
their light dissolving on our skin.

If this is damnation—let it be endless.
Let the night never end, let the music keep playing,
until time itself forgets the melody
and we remain—two notes dissonant in the black,
the eternal nocturne, still unfinished.

OBSIDIAN LAMENT

The river runs black,
its surface broken by unseen currents.
I lean over, tracing its reflection—
my face a twin of shadow and longing.

Above me, the sky is a cathedral of frost,
its stars sharpened like obsidian knives.
The wind bites at my throat,
bringing the smell of rain on cindered earth
and the faintest whiff of your absence.

I whisper into the dark—
the syllables hang like smoke,
folding themselves into the water,
into the trees, into the stone.

Somewhere, somewhere, it gathers—
the residue of all that was luminous,
all that remains unbroken
in the hollow of our devotion.

WHISPERS OF THE HOLLOW MOON

The crescent moon hangs low, a sickle of silver—
its light slicing the black velvet of night.
I move through the shadows of your absence,
my fingers, tracing the cold shape of memory.

Owls chant our names in the hollows,
their wings stirring forgotten secrets.
Gossamer-winged cecropia
flutter between us like fragile promises.

I speak to the stars—
to the unseen currents running beneath the world—
and every word bows toward you,
every breath calls you back
from the edge of the dark.

Even the soil remembers your weight—
soft impressions that bloom
with the scent of decay and devotion.
I kneel there, a pilgrim to your shadow,
and the night hums in answer—
a song only we can hear.

THE LAST ILLUMINATION

At the edge of all things, we lingered—
two silhouettes against the dying sky.
The stars had grown weary of burning,
their shimmer dimmed to a whisper of gold.

Your hand found mine—no need for words.
The air itself seemed to listen,
as if the universe feared to disturb
whatever we were becoming.

The wind moved through us like memory—
soft, deliberate, sacred.
I could taste the cosmos on your breath,
that delicate flavor of ending and beginning.

Below, the earth slept—
veins of root and ember entwined.
Above, the heavens trembled—
unraveling their constellations
to weave new ones in our shape.

I thought: this is how light survives—
not in the stars,
but in the spaces between two souls
who refuse to vanish.

And when you held me—
time folded, gently, inward.
All the darkness we had known
became illumination.

THE EARTH'S MEMORY

Hidden below the marrow of the world,
the roots whisper in tongues older than time.
Their sap runs black and glistening—
a hymn of hunger, a pulse of forgotten gods.

I pressed my hand to the earth
and felt it answer—
a slow, deliberate throb,
as though the planet itself remembered my name.

Above, the stars bled titanium,
their light thin and uncertain.
But down here—
everything gleamed in secrecy.

You came to me through the moss and stone,
your shadow dressed in moonlight,
your breath heavy with rain and ruin.

We spoke in silence—
only the soil understood.
Our hearts, twin embers buried deep,
burned through the centuries between us.

And when I touched you,
the ground shuddered—
veins of obsidian unfurled beneath us,
a black river binding bone to bone,
soul to soul.

Now every time it storms,
I hear that heartbeat again—
slow, eternal, patient—
as if the earth still dreams of us
in its dark, unbroken sleep.

SUGARED SIGHS

Through the labyrinthine hedgerows we glided—
our fingers entwined, tracing the curves of sun-warmed stone.
Amber light pooled through the leaves in broken streams,
and dragonflies hovered between the branches,
their wings stirring the scent of rain and fern.

The wind carried whispers of crushed thyme and soil,
drifting over roots and fallen leaves.
Petrichor and hidden resin wafted on the wind—
weaving a quiet spell around our bodies,
an unspoken promise written in shadow and captured gazes.

A sly, red fox padded through the misted hollows,
his eyes like moons reflecting our beacon of love.
We moved in tandem, a mirrored rhythm of heart and breath—
enveloping the night around us as if it were a lost letter,
each step a stanza, each glance a muted verse of eternity.

You breathed a sugared sigh that brushed my earlobe—
a benediction whispered into the garden's quiet pulse.
Every moment we shared seeped into the edges of the night,
our adoration etched into shadow and leaf—
and the air wisped, as if directing the pulse of our hearts.

THE SOFT-BLOOMING NIGHT

Mushrooms rise like lanterns
scattered by a moon that wandered off—
milk-white, breathing faint light
into the velvet moss.

Every step stirs something small.
A flutter of leaves.
A silver vole vanishing,
a fern lifting its green eyelash to the night.

Here, even the darkness feels alive—
gentle, watchful,
recognizing you as one of its own
and parting just enough
to let you through.

BRANDY LANE

THE WOODLAND'S REPLY

The forest feels your footsteps
long before you arrive—
a soft vibration threading through root and moss,
stirring the luminescent caps
in a slow, shimmering breath.

The ferns unfurl
as if waking for you,
as if some quiet instinct
remembers your light.

A moth drifts near your brow,
circling once, twice,
deciding you are safe—
that you belong to the hush
as much as any creature born beneath it.

Even the shadows surround you.
Not to frighten—
but to listen.
To cradle the shape of you
in their gentle, breathing dark.

Here, you are not a visitor.
You are the pulse moving through the night.
You are the reason the lanterns bloom.

THE BRAMBLE GATE

A knot of thorn and vine
marks the doorway to the deeper wood,
where paths forget themselves
and the world begins to sing softly.

Clusters of mushrooms bloom beneath—
cream, rust, indigo—
a quiet chorus glowing softly
at the forest's hem.

Something slips through the underbrush:
the brush of a fox tail,
the quick-footed hush of a rabbit,
wings folding like secrets against the dark.

Nothing here is afraid.
The woodland simply watches—
polite, patient,
ancient.

34

WALK BESIDE ME

The bramble parts more gently
when you are near—
as if the thorns remember softness
and step aside to let us pass.

Mushrooms grow in quiet clusters,
their light warming to your presence,
casting small halos on your hands
when our fingers brush in the dim.

Every creature hears us coming—
a fox slipping into shade,
a rabbit pausing mid-flight,
the brief flutter of wings settling above—
yet, nothing scatters in fear.
The woodland is listening, enchanted.

You tilt your head toward me,
and the world stills.
The vines seem to come closer,
eager to learn the shape
of what moves between us.

In this deep realm of the hidden path,
love feels inevitable—
a natural phenomenon,
like the luminescent creatures of night.

Here, under the bramble gate,
I swear the forest brightens
just to see you.

WHERE ROOTS REMEMBER

Old trees sway together—like ancestors
whispering through rings of time,
their roots knuckled deep
into soil dark as dusky water.

Mushrooms luminesce in their shade—
as though stirred by a memory
the Earth once held close
and never spoke again.

Creatures scurry in brief flashes;
a mouse, a beetle, the gray-furred slip
of a possum carrying her children to safety.
Each movement older than your heartbeat.
Each shadow, familiar.

36

BRANDY LANE

BENEATH THE ELDERS

When you step into the grove,
everything stills—
recognizing the quiet spark
that moves between us.

Mushrooms glow at our feet,
their light gathering around you
as if the earth remembers your name.

Your hand finds mine,
and the roots beneath us shift—
welcoming,
as though love itself
is part of their long memory.

In this hush of moss and shadow,
even the smallest creature pauses,
bearing witness
to something timeless.

Here, beneath the elders,
we belong.

THE MOTHWAY

A narrow trail curls through
the underbrush,
lit only by drifting moths—
their wings soft as breath,
carrying a pale, trembled light
like folded prayers.

Below them,
mushrooms mirror the glow.
Little moons pressed to the ground,
patient, listening.
A deer breaks cover—
a single startled breath
unraveling the silence.

The night rearranges itself
around the sound,
then settles again, forgiving.

BRANDY LANE

YOUR LIGHT IN THE DARK

Along the mothlit trail,
your shoulder brushes mine—
a small, steady warmth
in the trembling glow of their wings.

The fairy fire brightens at our passing,
tiny moons rising for you,
as if the night recognizes
the gentleness you carry.

A deer pauses in the hush,
listening to our shared breath,
our quiet laughter
folding itself into the dark.

And suddenly the path
doesn't feel narrow at all.
It widens around us—
soft, shimmering—
as if the whole forest
is guiding us forward.

Here, in this drifting light,
I see you clearly.
You are the lantern
the night has been saving
for me.

The Burrow Lanterns

Beyond the fallen cedar,
blue Mycena bloom in a perfect ring—
luminescent, trembling—
a quiet vigil kept for whatever creature
sleeps in the burrow at their center.

You hear the faintest scuffle:
a whisper of claws on soft soil.

A badger, perhaps.
A fawn.
Something warm, tucked deep
in the midnight earth.

The woodland does not explain.
It simply glows.
It simply keeps watch.

40

IN THE QUIET

The ring of mushrooms brightens
when you draw close—
their pale light gathering around us
like a secret they're willing to share.

Some small creature stirs in the burrow,
but even it stays calm,
as if your presence carries
its own kind of shelter.

You slip your hand into mine,
and the night settles deeper—
warm, familiar,
glowing gently at the edges.

Here, beside the hidden heartbeat
of the woodland,
I realize the truth of it:
I feel safest
where you are.

THE WATERFALL'S PROMISE

A thin waterfall threads down the rocks,
silver and steady,
its voice; filling the clearing
with a soft, unbroken hush.

Some small creature stirs in the underbrush,
then stills again
when you step beside me—
as if even the woodland recognizes
the gentleness between us.

Mist gathers on your hair,
catching the dim light
like scattered stars.
When you take my hand,
the whole forest exhales—
calm, whole, listening.

The water glides over stone,
a quiet reminder
that everything finds its way home
eventually.

And standing here with you,
I know this:
In the shelter of falling water
and trembling leaves,
love feels as natural
as breath—
soft as the river's promise,
and just as certain.

THE MOON'S PULSE

Above the garden path,
the moon hangs low—
a silver ache hanging
on the edge of the sky.
Starlight collects on your skin,
soft as fingertips tracing
the quiet lines of desire.

You step closer,
and the night seems to deepen around us—
a single breath drawn in
by all of nature.
Your gaze meets mine, warm, certain,
and the air shifts—
charged, waiting.

Overhead, the stars burn slowly,
bright enough to reveal
the curve of your mouth,
the way your eyes soften
when the world falls away.

44

The moonlight slips across your shoulders,
down your throat,
resting in the hollow
where my gaze lingers too long.
You don't look away.
Neither do I.

Here, in this dark clearing,
with the moon spilling like liquid silver,
I feel the gravity of you—
pulling, steady, sure—
a quiet desire
written in light.

And when you hold me close,
the whole night holds still,
as though every star
has paused its burning
just to watch us.

CECROPIA

Night lifts its velvet wings,
and there you are—
a hush of rust and cream,
patterned with whispers
I can almost read.

Your body swells with quiet power,
antennae like delicate fans
catching the unseen vibrations
of the world around you.

You drift through the dark,
a soft beacon
that does not burn,
that does not ask for anything
but the space to exist.

I watch you disappear into the night,
wings trembling like a secret,
and I imagine
how it must feel
to know the sky
and carry it
on your own quiet back.

Even the leaves curl,
breath held,
as if the forest knows
it is witnessing
something reverent,
fragile,
and impossible
to hold.

HOMEWARD

The night releases you slowly,
like a breath it has been holding.
Stars soften.
The trees loosen their dark embrace.

You follow the quiet path back—
heart still glowing
with everything you met
in the hush between shadows.

And when the first hint of dawn
touches your skin,
you realize:

You didn't leave the reverie behind.
It followed you home—
settling into the tender spaces
you carry everywhere.

BRANDY LANE

THE FOREST COMES HOME

You open the door
and the night comes quietly with you—
the scent of cedar in your hair,
the hush of leaves still clinging
to your breath.

Moonlight settles on your forehead
like it recognizes
its favorite place to rest.

You move through your rooms
softly,
carrying the forest in your pulse—
a little wildness,
a little wonder,
still glowing beneath your skin.

And somehow,
the house feels wider tonight,
as though it, too, has learned
to breathe like the trees.

HOME *sweet* HOME

HEARTHSONG

Even inside,
the forest finds you—
a stray feather on the floor,
a cool breeze slipping past the curtains
with the quiet confidence
of an old friend.

You light a candle,
and it flickers the same gentle way
a firefly does
when it's deciding
whether to trust your hand.

The world grows small and warm.
Your heart grows wide and wild.

And in that moment,
you understand:
Home is not the walls around you,
but the place where nature
rests without fear—
in your breath,
in your bones,
in the soft rhythm
of your becoming.

ABOUT THE AUTHOR

BRANDY LANE

Brandy Lane does not merely write poetry—she lives within it. Her heart is a shoreline where words crash like waves, carrying shells of memory, sea-glass dreams, and salt-sweet confessions. Each poem she writes is a tide, each collection a vessel of longing and light. In *Where Beautiful Loves I & II, The Briny Sea of Poetry, Unrequited, Talking to the Moon,* and *The Corset and The Loom,* she traces the fragile architecture of the heart, mapping desire, loss, hope, and the raw intensity of living fully.

But her voice is not hers alone. Brandy gathers the voices of others as one gathers wildflowers, binding them into anthologies that breathe. *In Love is Pain (Volumes 1 and 2)* and *Winter,* she brings together poets from every corner of the globe, from every walk of life, shaping a garden where tenderness and ache bloom side by side. Through her imprint, **Where Beautiful Inks LLC**, she has published Stevie Flood, Anila Bukhari, and DM Takeshi, and served as publishing consultant and formatter for Angela Psalm under **The Dungeon Keep Atheneum** in Australia, as well as for Diane Lipton Gollub. Every book, every anthology, every line she shepherds carries her deep devotion to the craft, the artist, and the act of creation itself.

Her poetry has appeared in more than forty anthologies and literary magazines worldwide, including *Poetry 365, Poetica 2 and 3, Through the Looking Glass, But You Don't Look Sick, Red Penguin Books' The Flower Shop on the Corner and The Ocean Waves, As Darkness Falls,* and many more. She appears in *Who's Who of Emerging Writers,* and continues to illuminate the spaces between sorrow and joy, absence and beauty, in both print and digital forms.

Brandy lives in Indiana, where the world around her pulses with energy, movement, and creativity, a constant companion to her writing and publishing. She can be found on Instagram @wherebeautifullives, leaving traces of her journey—sun-washed images, moonlit lines, and glimpses into the spaces where beauty waits. Her work, and the voices she nurtures, can also be explored through her Canva website linked on her Instagram page.

In every act of creation—whether writing, publishing, or guiding other voices—Brandy Lane shapes a world where poetry is not just read, but lived, felt, and remembered.

www.ingramcontent.com/pod-product-compliance
Lightning Source LLC
Chambersburg PA
CBHW051334120626
46547CB00016B/2533